Pebble® Plus

CARS, CARS, CARS

FAMOUS CARS

by Melissa Abramovitz

Gail Saunders-Smith, PhD, Consulting Editor

Consultant: Leslie Mark Kendall, Curator
Petersen Automotive Museum
Los Angeles, California

CAPSTONE PRESS
a capstone imprint

Pebble Plus is published by Capstone Press,
1710 Roe Crest Drive, North Mankato, Minnesota 56003.
www.capstonepub.com

Library of Congress Cataloging-in-Publication Data
Abramovitz, Melissa, 1954–
 Famous cars / by Melissa Abramovitz.
    p. cm.—(Pebble plus. Cars, cars, cars)
 Summary: "Simple text and color photographs describe nine famous cars"—Provided by the publisher.
 Audience: K-3.
 Includes bibliographical references and index.
 ISBN 978-1-62065-091-2 (library binding)
 ISBN 978-1-62065-871-0 (paperback)
 ISBN 978-1-4765-1073-6 (eBook PDF)
 1. Automobiles—Juvenile literature. 2. Automobiles in mass media—Juvenile literature. I. Title. II. Series: Pebble plus. Cars, cars, cars.
 TL147.A278 2013
 629.222—dc23   2012031831

Editorial Credits
Erika L. Shores; Kyle Grenz, designer; Laura Manthe, production specialist

Photo Credits
Alamy: AF Archive, 7; Getty Images: Silver Screen Collection, 5; Landov: NTI/Lee Sanders, 11; Newscom: Splash News/RM Auctions, 19, Splash News/Solent News, 9, WENN.com/ZOB/JP5, 17, ZUMA Press, 15; Rex Features via AP Images, cover (top); The Kobal Collection/Warner Bros, 13; Wikimedia/Photo by Jennifer Graylock/Ford Motor Company, cover (bottom), 21

Artistic Effects
Shutterstock: 1xpert

Note to Parents and Teachers

The Cars, Cars, Cars set supports national science standards related to science, technology, and society. This book describes and illustrates famous cars. The images support early readers in understanding the text. The repetition of words and phrases helps early readers learn new words. This book also introduces early readers to subject-specific vocabulary words, which are defined in the Glossary section. Early readers may need assistance to read some words and to use the Table of Contents, Glossary, Read More, Internet Sites, and Index sections of the book.

Printed in the United States of America in North Mankato, Minnesota.
092012   006933CGS13

Table of Contents

Four-Wheeled Stars!

They're magical, funny,

or filled with cool tools.

These cool cars are stars!

Chitty Chitty Bang Bang thinks,

floats, and flies.

Chitty takes the Potts family

on an exciting trip.

Chitty Chitty Bang Bang is a custom-made 1910-era race car.

The Flintstones' car doesn't
have doors, a floor,
or an engine. Passengers' feet
move this rock and wood car.

The Flintstones' car is a
Hanna-Barbera cartoon car.

Doc Brown's DeLorean becomes

a time machine at 88 miles

(142 kilometers) per hour.

A make-believe "flux capacitor"

helps send passengers back in time.

**The "Back to the Future"
DeLorean is a 1981 DMC-12.**

Movie and TV Race Cars

Herbie the Love Bug drives himself,
skips across lakes, and does
wheelies. Herbie's not a race car.
But his friend is a race car driver.
Herbie helps his friend win races.

Herbie is a 1963 Volkswagen Sunroof Beetle.

Bulletproof shields and

jump jacks give Mach 5 an edge.

Speed Racer and Mach 5 beat

the bad guys and win the big race.

Mach 5 is a custom-made race car.

Famous race car Lightning McQueen

finds new friends in Radiator Springs.

McQueen learns that friendship

and kindness are what make

a true winner.

Lightning McQueen is a Disney-Pixar "Cars" cartoon race car.

Superheroes' Cars

The Ghostbusters' Ecto-1 carries
proton packs and a roof rack
with other tools. A siren warns
that the Ghostbusters are
on their way!

Ecto-1 is a 1959 Cadillac Miller-Meteor ambulance.

Machine guns! Oil sprayers!

A button sends unwanted

passengers through the roof.

An Aston Martin keeps

secret agent James Bond safe.

The first Bond car was a 1963 Aston Martin DB5.

The bulletproof Batmobile
helps Batman fight crime.
KAPOW! Its rockets blast
the bad guys.

A custom-made 1955 Lincoln Futura was the first Batmobile.

Glossary

bulletproof—something that has been made to protect people from bullets

custom-made—built for a certain reason

engine—a machine that makes the power needed to move something

flux capacitor—the make-believe device that lets the DeLorean travel in time

jump jack—a spring that lets Mach 5 jump over things

Mach—a unit of measurement for speeds faster than the speed of sound

passenger—someone besides the driver who rides in a vehicle

proton pack—a backpack worn by the Ghostbusters that shoots out a make-believe proton beam to stop ghosts

secret agent—someone who gets secrets from another government

siren—a device that makes a loud sound

wheelie—raising the front wheels of a vehicle off the ground

Read More

Doman, Mary Kate. *Cool Cars.* All about Big Machines. Berkeley Heights, N.J.: Enslow Elementary, 2012.

Harrison, Emma. *Herbie Fully Loaded Official Movie Scrapbook.* New York: Disney Press, 2005.

Kelly, Sophia. *Speed Racer: The Official Racing Book.* New York: Price Stern Sloan, 2008.

Internet Sites

FactHound offers a safe, fun way to find Internet sites related to this book. All of the sites on FactHound have been researched by our staff.

Here's all you do:

Visit *www.facthound.com*

Type in this code: 9781620650912

Super-cool stuff! Check out projects, games and lots more at www.capstonekids.com

Index

Word Count: 209
Grade: 1
Early-Intervention Level: 23